Prayers of the Heart

✦   ✦   ✦

Prayers of the Heart

✦ ✦ ✦

Marla D. Whittington

authorHOUSE®

AuthorHouse™
1663 Liberty Drive
Bloomington, IN 47403
www.authorhouse.com
Phone: 1-800-839-8640

Published by AuthorHouse   11/27/2012

ISBN: 978-1-4772-9216-7 (sc)
ISBN: 978-1-4772-9215-0 (e)

Library of Congress Control Number: 2012921865

Any people depicted in stock imagery provided by Thinkstock are models, and such images are being used for illustrative purposes only. Certain stock imagery © Thinkstock.

This book is printed on acid-free paper.

Because of the dynamic nature of the Internet, any web addresses or links contained in this book may have changed since publication and may no longer be valid. The views expressed in this work are solely those of the author and do not necessarily reflect the views of the publisher, and the publisher hereby disclaims any responsibility for them.

Bible quotations are taken from the Thomas Nelson King James version, KJV copyright 1988 by Thomas Nelson, Inc.

Scripture references marked TAB are taken from the Amplified Bible version copyright 1965 by Zondervon Publishing House.

Contents

✦ ✦ ✦

Effectual Prayers

Decrees

DEDICATION

✦ ✦ ✦

First and foremost, I dedicate this book to my Lord and Savior Jesus Christ. Thank you for first loving me unconditionally, bringing restoration in my life by your Word, pouring your mercy and grace over me making me a woman of prayer. I could have not done this without you.

To my children, LuVince IV, LaTrice Nicolle, and Lamar Navelle whom I love so dearly. May these words bring unconditional love and understanding to your souls. To my six grandchildren, may these words bring wisdom and direction to your lives.

To my sister Anita and my brother Darnell, may these words free your mind and bring peace and restoration to your souls, and to a special friend, Gloria Clayton, thank you for encouraging me to write this book and for showing me a mother's love.

INTRODUCTION
✦ ✦ ✦

These prayers have been compiled from the Word of God. It's in times like this, you need a sure way to change your situations. "God's people" have been oppressed, lied to, tricked, and things stolen by the enemy.

Jesus used His spoken word to cast out devils, to raise the dead, to heal the sick and to defeat Satan. When the enemy comes over your children, families; marriages, finances and jobs, etc. the bible says, *"The Word of God is quick and powerful and sharper than any two edged sword."* Hebrews 4:12 You have to remember all the power you have in you that you can tread upon serpents and scorpions and over all the power of the enemy and nothing shall by any means hurt you. These words are God's word to be used for your personal use, in your relationships in the Body of Christ when the enemy comes in like a flood, and to remind you what Christ's love did for you.

God wants you to use His word, apply His word, and pray His word to help you through your daily lives. This is your responsibility as Christians and to our Lord and Savior Jesus Christ.

We are not to judge one another lest we be judged for the same judgment. In this day and time we are dealing with issues of the heart from our past, finances, families, church and relationships. Christians have been under heavy oppression by the enemy and feeling as though they have been pushed down spiritually. You have been repressed in your spirit to the point you have no freedom to freely praise and worship God.

These scriptural prayers, petitions, promises and confessions are to guide you in to the presence of God and give you a complete breakthrough from Satan, his attacks, and to bombard the heavenlies for a release of the promises and blessings for your life.

The church of Jesus Christ must have a priority of prayer right now. It has never been a greater time when the world has needed God. People are in fear and uncertainty everywhere. Many countries and nations are living in chaos of economic collapse with millions of people living in poverty and starvation. The cities are plagued with violence, pornography, prostitution, drugs, and crime. Our children are not safe on the playgrounds. At schools; they have become prey for pedophiles and can't even play in their own backyards. Homosexuality is being considered as an alternate lifestyle, and gay marriages are accepted. Television openly portrays it. There are people around us on our jobs, in our neighborhoods, friends, and relatives who are not saved and who are bound with sickness, disease, and tormented by the oppressor, the devil.

Therefore also now, saith the LORD, "Turn ye even to me with all your heart, and with fasting, and with weeping, and with mourning: And rend your heart, and not your garments, and turn unto the LORD your God," for he is gracious and merciful, slow to anger, and of great kindness, and repent him of the evil. Blow the trumpet in Zion, sanctify yourselves, fast, and call a solemn assembly: Gather the people, sanctify the congregation, assemble the elders, gather the children, and those that suck the breasts: let the bridegroom go forth of his chamber, and the bride out of her closet. Let the priests, the ministers of the LORD, weep between the porch and the altar, and let them say, Spare thy people, O LORD, and give not your heritage to reproach, that the heathen should rule over them: wherefore should they say among the people, Where is their God? Then will the LORD be jealous for his land, and pity his people. He will no more make you a reproach among the heathen. Fear not, O land; be glad and rejoice: for the LORD will do great things be glad then, you children of Zion, and rejoice in the LORD your God: for he hath given you the former rain moderately, and he will cause to come down for you the rain, the former rain, and the latter rain in the first month. And the floors shall be full of wheat, and the vats shall overflow with wine and oil. And I will restore to you the years that the locust hath eaten, the cankerworm, and the caterpillar, and the palmerworm, my great army which I sent among you. And ye shall eat in plenty, and be satisfied, and praise the name of the LORD your God that has dealt wondrously with you: and my people shall never be ashamed.

May God grant you out of the rich treasures of His heart to be strengthened and reinforced with mighty power in the inner man by the Holy Spirit. May Christ through your faith actually dwell, settle down, abide, and make his permanent home in your hearts! May you be rooted deep in love and founded securely on love that you may have the power and be strong to apprehend and grasp with all the saints to be filled unto all the fullness of God that you may have the rich measures of the divine present and become wholly filled and flooded with God himself. May the LORD bless thee, and keep thee: May the LORD make his face shine upon thee, and be gracious unto thee: and may the LORD lift up his countenance upon thee, and give thee peace.

Preparation for the Battle
✦ ✦ ✦

The Armour of God

Submit yourselves therefore to God, resist the devil. And he will flee from you. James 4:7 KJV

Paul said, "Therefore put on God's complete armour that you may be able to resist and stand your ground on the evil day (of danger) and having done all the (crises demand) to stand firmly in your place." Eph 6:16 TAB

Take possession of the victory for the battle has already been won, so put on the whole armour of God for protection; for we wrestle not against flesh and blood, but against principalities, against powers, against the rulers of the darkness of this world, against spiritual wickedness in high places.

Wherefore I will take unto me the whole armour of God that I may be able to withstand in the evil day, and having done all to stand.

Stand therefore, having my loins girted about with truth, and having on the breast plate of righteous; and my feet shod with the preparation of the gospel of peace; above all taking the

1

shield of faith, wherewith I shall be able to quench all the fiery darts of the wicked. I will take the helmet of salvation, and the sword of the spirit, which is the word of God: Praying always with all prayer and supplication in the spirit, and watching there unto with all perseverance and supplication for all saints; and for me, that utterance may be given unto me, that I may open my mouth boldly, to make known the mystery of the gospel, and put Satan away from my family, finances and friends. In Jesus name Amen.

I Corinthians 6

✦ ✦ ✦

Hear the right, O Lord, attend unto my cry, and give ear unto my prayer.

I acknowledge my sin unto you, and my iniquities I have not hid. I will confess my transgressions unto the Lord and he will forgive the iniquity of my sin. I repent for committing fornication. I know that my body is not for fornication, but for the Lord, and the Lord for the body. I repent for covetousness. I know your commandment says, "I should not covet." I repent for being an extortionist. I know that I should be content with what I have, and that the love of money is the root of all evil. I repent for being an idolater. Lord, I will put away strange gods I will not provoke you to jealousy. I repent for being a railer. I will not let Satan get an advantage over me for I am not ignorant of his devices. I repent for drunkenness. I will take heed to myself unless at any time my heart is over charged with excess and drunkenness and cares of this life, and so that day comes upon me unaware. I repent for committing adultery. I will rise and pray unless I enter into temptation. I know if I commit adultery I lack understanding, and if I do it, I will destroy my own soul.

I repent for being effeminate and an abuser of myself with mankind. I know that God will give me up to uncleanness through the lust of my own heart, to dishonor my own body between myself. I repent for being a thief. I know that if a man be found stealing, then that thief should die and evil will be put away from among him. Father, I know that only the righteous shall inherit the kingdom of God, and I was bought with a price; therefore, I will glorify God in my body and spirit which are God's. In Jesus name Amen.

GALATIANS 5

✦ ✦ ✦

Judge me, O Lord, for I have walked in my own integrity. Examine me, Lord, prove me, try my reins and my heart.

I will walk in the spirit; I will not fulfill the lust of the flesh.

I repent for committing adultery. I know that if I commit adultery and look on a man/woman to lust after him/her. I have committed adultery with him/her in my heart already.

I repent for fornication. I know that I should possess my vessel in sanctification and honor.

I repent for uncleanness. I know that God has not called us unto uncleanness, but unto holiness.

I repent for lasciviousness. I know that I should deny ungodliness and worldly lust living sober, righteously and Godly in this present world.

I repent for witchcraft. I know that all who do these things are an abomination unto the Lord, and because of these abominations, the Lord our God will drive them out before him.

I repent for hatred. I know that I should not hate. If I am angry with my brethren without a cause, I shall be in danger of judgment.

I repent for variance. Search me, O God, and know my heart. Try me and know my Thought. See if there be any wicked way in me and lead me in the way everlasting.

I repent for emulations. I know that I am fearfully and wonderfully made and marvelous are your works.

I repent for wrath. I know that I can be angry, but do not sin and do not let the sun go down on my wrath.

I repent for strife. I am to pursue peace with all men and be a minister of reconciliation.

I repent for seditions. I know that my speech should always be with grace, and seasoned with salt that I may know how I ought to answer every man.

I repent for heresies. I have turned my ears for the truth and listened to fables. I will do what is written in your Word that I might have the Tree of Life.

I repent for being envious. I know that I should prove my own works and rejoice in myself alone and not in another.

I repent for murder. I know that a murderer shall surely be put to death.

I repent for drunkenness. I will not be drunk with wine, wherein is excess, but filled with the spirit for this body is the temple of God.

I repent for revelling's. I will walk in integrity and let uprightness preserve me.

O Lord, help me not to do these things or anything such like them, for if I do these things, I will not inherit the kingdom of God. Hide my face from my sin and blot out all my iniquities. Create in me a clean heart and renew a right spirit within me.

In Jesus name Amen.

MARK 7

✦   ✦   ✦

The heart is deceitful and above all things desperately wicked, who can know it.

I know there is nothing from without a man that entering into him can defile him, but the things which comes out of him, those are the things which defile a man.

Father, it's against you and you only that I have sinned and do this evil in your sight that you might be justified when you speak and be clear when you judge. Create in me a clean heart and renew a right spirit within me.

Father, I repent for having evil thoughts. I know that you are angry with the wicked every day. I will think on things that are of a good report, if there be any virtue if there be any praise, I will think on these things.

I repent for committing adultery. I know that is the commandment of the law. I will govern my mind and body accordingly to follow all your commandments.

I repent for committing fornication. I know that my body is the temple of the Holy Spirit and for the Lord and the Lord for my body.

I repent for being a murderer. I know that this the works of the flesh; deliver me from blood guiltiness, O God of my salvation. I will let all bitterness, wrath, anger, clamour and evil speaking be put away from me.

I repent for committing thefts. I know that I should not give place to the devil, but rather labor working with my hands that thing which is good, that I may have to give to him that needs.

I repent for being covetous. I know that this is a law of the commandments, and I don't want to be a transgressor of the law.

I repent for wickedness. Lord, deliver me from evil. I know that the dwelling place of the wicked shall come to naught. I repent for being deceitful. I know that this is an evil treasure coming from my heart.

I will love the Lord with all my heart, and all my soul, all my mind, and with all my strength.

I repent for lasciviousness. I will flee from my youthful lusts, but follow righteousness, faith, charity, peace and call upon the Lord out of a pure heart.

I repent for an evil eye. I will not be wise in my own eyes, but fear the Lord and depart from evil.

I repent for blasphemy. I know that this is an unpardonable sin; I will walk in the spirit and not in my flesh. I repent for pride. I know prides goes before destruction and a haughty spirit before a fall.

I repent for foolishness. I know that a fool is right in his own eyes. I will walk with integrity and let uprightness preserve me.

All these things are evil that come from within and defile a man. Lord, instruct me and teach me in the way which I shall go, guide me with your eye, hide your word in my heart that I may not sin against you. In Jesus name. Amen.

PROVERBS 6

✝   ✝   ✝

Father, I acknowledge my sin unto you, and my iniquities I have not hid. I will confess my transgression unto you Lord, and you will forgive my iniquity of my sin.

I repent for a proud look, thinking of myself higher than I ought to. I repent of a lying tongue. I will put away lying and speak truth to everyman.

I repent for using my hands to shed innocent blood, which is the works of my flesh.

I repent for my heart that devises wicked imaginations. I know my heart is deceitful above all things and desperately wicked.

I repent for my feet swift in running to mischief; for I know that the law is not made for a righteous man but for the lawless and disobedient. I repent for being a false witness that speaks lies; I know that my tongue can no man tame. It is an unruly evil, full of deadly poison.

I repent for sowing discord among my brethren. I know that I will not let corrupt communication proceed out of my mouth, but let that which is good to the use of edifying that it may minister grace to the hearers.

Father I know that these are the six things that you hate and the seventh one is an abomination to you. Help me to keep your commandments and forsake not to walk in your statutes. Bind them continually upon my heart that I may not sin against you. In Jesus name Amen!

Revelations 21

✦ ✦ ✦

Father, for I acknowledge my transgressions, and my sin is ever before me. It's against you and only you have I sinned and done this evil in your sight, that you might be justified when You speak and be clear when You judge. I believe that in the beginning was the Word, and the Word was with God, and the Word was God. The same was in the beginning with God. All things were made by Him, and without Him was not anything made that was made. In Him was life; and the life was the light of men.

I repent for being fearful. Lord, you are my light and my salvation of whom shall I fear. I repent for being unbelieving. I know that only the righteous shall see God. For whosoever shall call upon the name of the Lord shall be saved. I repent for committing an abomination; I know that the judgment of God is that they which commit such things are worthy of death. I repent for being a murderer; I know that this is the work of the flesh. I repent for being a whoremonger. I will put away the lust of my flesh and possess my vessel in sanctification and honor. I repent for any sorcery and divination. I will submit myself unto God and resist the devil and he will flee from me. I repent for

15

being a liar. I know that if I have clean hands and a pure heart I will have the right to the Tree of Life.

Thank you, Father, that if I overcome all these things, I shall inherit the kingdom of heaven, and you will be my God, and I shall be your people. In Jesus name Amen

ROMANS 1

✝ ✝ ✝

Blessed is he whose transgression is forgiven and whose sin is covered. Blessed is the man unto whom the Lord does not impute iniquity. Father, I repent for being filled with all unrighteousness. I know that only the righteous shall see God.

I repent for committing fornication. I know that it is your will for me to abstain from fornication and present my body a living sacrifice holy and acceptable unto you.

I repent for wickedness. Cleanse my heart from my secret faults.

I repent for being covetous. I know that there is no temptation taken me, but as such as is common to man, but God is faithful, who will not let me be tempted above that which I am able, but will with the temptation also make a way to escape that I may bear it.

I repent for being malicious. I know that vengeance is the Lords, he will repay; he will fight my battles.

I repent for being envious. I will meditate on your precepts, O Lord, deliver my soul.

I repent for being a murderer. I know that this is the works of my flesh; deliver me from blood guiltiness, oh God of my salvation.

I repent for debating. I know that I should not let any corrupt communication proceed out of my mouth.

I repent for being deceitful. Judge me, O God, and plead my cause against an ungodly nation, deliver me from being an unjust man.

I repent for malignity. I know that if I hate, I will be clothed with shame.

I repent for being a whisperer and a backbiter. I know that this is inexcusable. Who am I to judge, for if I judge another, I condemn myself.

I repent for hating God. How much more shall the blood of Christ, who through eternal Spirit offer himself without spot to God. I will purge my conscience from dead works to serve the living God.

I repent for being despiteful. I know the Lord will abhor the bloody and deceitful man.

I repent for being proud and boastful. I know that only by pride comes contention, but with well advised wisdom.

I repent for being an inventor of evil. I know that I am cursed if I do wickedness. I will serve the Lord with my whole heart.

I repent for being disobedient to my parents. I will obey my parent (s) in the Lord for this is right, and my days will be long on the earth.

I repent for being without understanding. I know the fear of the Lord is the beginning of wisdom and the knowledge of the holy is understanding.

I repent for being a covenant breaker. I will meditate on the book of the law day and night that I may observe to do according to all that is written therein.

I repent for not having natural affection. I know that this is an abomination unto the Lord and the person(s) who commit them shall be cut off from among their people. I will be kindly affectionate one to another with brotherly love.

I repent for being implacable. I know that I shall not give place to the devil; that I am to resist him and he will flee from me.

I repent for being unmerciful. I know that if I am merciful I will obtain mercy and be blessed.

Father, I know the judgment of God, that they which commit such things are worthy of death. Purge me with hyssop and I shall be clean. Wash me, and I shall be whiter than snow. Create in me a clean heart, O God, and renew a right spirit within me. In Jesus name Amen.

Ten Commandments

✦ ✦ ✦

Search me, O God, and know my heart. Try me and know my thoughts, and see if there is any wicked way in me, and lead me in the way of everlasting. Wash me thoroughly from my iniquity, and cleanse me from my sin. For I acknowledge my transgressions, and my sin is ever before me. It's against you, only you, have I sinned and done this evil in your sight that you might be justified when you speak and be clear when you judge.

Purge me with hyssop, and I shall be clean, wash me, and I shall be whiter than snow.

Create in me a clean heart, O God, and renew a right spirit within me.

Lord, you have commanded me in your word, that I shall not have any other gods before you. I shall not make unto me any graven images or any likeness of such things that is in heaven above or that is in the earth beneath or that is in the water under the earth. I shall not bow down myself to them nor serve them. I repent, for this is idolatry. I know that you are a jealous God, that every knee must bow and every tongue must confess that Jesus Christ is Lord.

I shall not take the Lords name in vain. I repent, and I know that you will not hold me guiltless if I take your name in vain. I have not remembered the Sabbath Day to keep it Holy. I repent, for hidding my eyes from your Sabbaths, and I will remember to keep them holy. I have not honored my father and mother. I repent, for cursing my father and mother for I shall surely be put to death, and that my days may not be long on the earth.

I shall not kill. I repent, because I know that I should not let any corrupt communication proceed out of my mouth, but that which is good to the use of edifying, that it may minister grace to the hearer, and if I smite anyone with an instrument of iron, or stone, or such thing wherewith he dies, I will surely be put to death.

I repent for committing adultery. I know that if a man be found lying with a married woman, with a husband both of them shall die. I shall not steal; I know that if I steal I will be cursed and cutoff from the Lord. I shall not bear false witness against my neighbor. I repent for, I know that a false witness shall not be unpunished, and he who speaks lies shall not escape. I shall not covet.

I repent, for I know that the blessing of the Lord makes it rich and he adds no sorrow to it. All unrighteous is sin. With my whole heart, I have sought you, O Lord, let me not wonder from your commandments, for this is the love of God that we keep his commandments. In Jesus name Amen.

II Timothy 3

✦ ✦ ✦

Father, I know also that in the last days perilous times shall come, for this shall everyone that is Godly pray unto you in a time when you may be found.

Father, I repent for being a lover of my own self; I know that pride goes before destruction and a haughty spirit before a fall. I repent for being covetous, I know that godliness with contentment is great gain, for I brought nothing into this world and it is certain I can carry nothing out. I repent for boasting, I know that if I keep my mouth and my tongue, I keep my soul from troubles.

I repent for being proud. I know that a man's pride shall bring him low, but honor shall uphold that humble in spirit. I repent for blasphemy. I know that whosoever speaks a word against the son of man, it shall be forgiven him, but whosoever speaks against the Holy Ghost, it shall not be forgiven him. I repent for being disobedient to my parents. I know that I am to obey them for this is right. I repent for being unthankful. I know that I should do to men what good they have done for me. I repent for being unholy. I know that I should be holy and without blame before God in love. I repent for being without natural affection. I know of my doings whether it is pure or whether it is right. I repent for being a truce breaker. I know that there is a way that seems right unto man, but the end thereof are the ways of death. I repent for being a false accuser. I know that lying lips are an abomination to the Lord, but they that deals truthfully are his delight. I repent for being incontent. I know that for the love of money is the root of all evil, which whiles some, coveted after, they have erred from the faith and pierced themselves through with many sorrows. I repent for being fierce. I know that he who has no rule covet his own spirit is like a city that is broken down and without walls.

I repent for being a despiser of those that are good. I know that if I hate my brother without a cause, I will be clothed with shame.

I repent for being a traitor. I know that I cannot be betwixt two opinions, either I love one or hate the other. I repent for being heady and high minded. I know that it is better to be of a humble spirit with the lowly than to divide the spoil with the proud. I repent for being a lover of pleasure more than a lover of God. I know that enjoying the pleasure of sin is for a season. In all this, Lord, I repent of having a form of godliness but denying the power thereof. I know that whosoever resists the power resists the ordinance of God, and they that resist shall receive to themselves damnation. I will be glad in the Lord and rejoice and shout for his deliverance. In Jesus name Amen!

TITHES & OFFERING
✦ ✦ ✦

Father, I acknowledge my sin unto you and my iniquity I have not hid. I will confess my transgression unto you, Lord. Wash me thoroughly from my iniquity and cleanse me from my sin.

From the days of my father, I have gone away from your ordinances, and I have not kept them. I will return unto you, Lord, through my tithes and offering. I will bring them into the storehouse that there may be meat in your house. I will prove you to see the windows of heaven will open up and pour me out a blessing that there shall not be room enough to receive. I will see you rebuke the devour, for my sake and all nations shall call me blessed; for I shall be a delightsome land. I shall be blessed in the city and I shall be blessed in the field. Blessed shall I be when I come in and blessed shall I be when I go out.

The Lord shall command the blessing upon me in my storehouse and in all that I set my hands to. The Lord shall establish an Holy people unto himself as he has sworn to us if we shall keep his commandments and walk in his ways. In Jesus name Amen.

Prayer for Addiction
+ + +

Father God, in the name of Jesus, I come to you with the authority and power you have given me to tread upon serpents and scorpions and over all the power of the enemy.

For though we walk in the flesh, we do not war after the flesh, for the weapons of our warfare are not carnal, but mighty through God to the pulling down of strong holds, casting down imaginations and every high thing that exalts itself against the knowledge of God, and bringing into captivity every thought into the obedience of Christ Jesus.

I renounce and cast down every evil influence and every satanic bondage of abuse that is binding me to the spirits of addiction.

I loose myself from the ruling sprits of nicotine, caffeine, cybersex, internet computer use, alcohol, gambling, cell phone use, video games, pornography, compulsive shopping, pills, sugar, exercise, compulsive eating, all drugs, lust, sex, pride, fear, anger, all hurt, pain, bound and blocked emotions, witchcraft, control and any connected related spirits that is causing these spirits to control my mind, body and soul.

Father, help me to surrender my will and fully trust you and only you and not myself.

Whatsoever I bind on earth shall be bound in heaven; whatsoever I loose on earth shall be loosed in heaven. I bind the spirits of rebellion, rejection, compulsion, covetousness, abuse, addiction, depression, mind control, suicide, rejection, selfishness, fear, lying spirits, stealing, uncontrollable sex drive, shame, depression and guilt in the name of Jesus. I submit my mind, body, emotions, eyes, ears, tongue, hands, feet and my entire sexual character to Jesus Christ. I loose the spirit of trust, peace, joy, love, hope, truth, meekness, faith, gentleness and goodness over my mind, body, spirit, soul, and life. I plead the blood of Jesus for my protection to help me not to be tempted, because God is faithful who will not let me be tempted above that which I am able, but will with the temptation also make a way to escape that I may bear it.

In Jesus name Amen!

Prayer Against Satan
+ + +

Father, in the name of Jesus, I thank you for suffering for me dying for me, redeeming me, so that I can be free from sin, sickness, diseases and the snares of Satan. He was a murderer from the beginning and abode not in the truth, because there is no truth in him, when he speaks a lie he speaks of his own, he is a liar and the father of it. For we wrestle not against flesh and blood, but against principalities, against powers, against the rulers of the darkness of this world, against spiritual wickedness in high places.

Father, help me (us) through the Holy Spirit to recognize the plans and plots of Satan, unless he should get an advantage of me (us), For I (we) are not ignorant of his devices, you gave me (us) all power over all the power of the enemy and nothing by any means shall hurt me (us).

The weapons of our warfare are not carnal, but mighty through God to the pulling down of strongholds casting down imaginations and every high thing that exalts itself against the knowledge of God.

Thank you, Lord, for the power and authority you have given me (us) to defeat Satan.

Greater is he that is in me, than he that is in the world. Now comes salvation and strength and the kingdom of God and the power of his Christ for the accuser of our brethren is cast down which accused us before our God day and night, and I (we) overcame him by the blood of the lamb and by the word of my (our) testimony.

I submit myself unto God and resist the devil, and he will flee from me (us). The God of peace shall bruise Satan under my (our) feet shortly. The grace of our Lord Jesus Christ be with me (us) Amen!

DELIVERANCE FROM HINDERING SPIRITS/DEMONIC FORCES

✦ ✦ ✦

Heavenly Father, when the enemy comes in like a flood, the spirits of the Lord will lift up a standard against him. I (we) ask that you would send your warring angels, that you would give me (us) power over all the power of the enemy. I (we) ask that you would prepare me (us) for the battle of the Lord, that I (we) would be fit for the battle of the Lord, that I (we) would be ready for the battle of the Lord, that you would make me (us) stand in the battle of the Lord, and that you would defend me (us) in the battle of the Lord.

May the Holy Spirit give me (us) discernment and empower my (our) gifts to set the captives free that you would block all transference of spirits assigned to hinder, stop or block me (us).

Father, I (we) ask that you will cut off all evil powers and influences directed toward me (us). Let every strongman present itself, all demonic door keepers be bound in Jesus name.

I (we) command all communication between the enemy forces be stopped and let confusion be loosed on them as with a mantle.

I (we) command all evil spirits to come out!

Let every lying spirit of unbelief, doubt, fear, deception, confusion and mind control spirits to be loosed in Jesus name.

Satan, I (we) renounce all your tactics, all evil spirits and activity from connected and related hindering spirits, and I (we) command these ruling spirits to go and be cast out and never return.

I (we) am covered with the blood of Jesus and I (we) loose peace and the spirit of God over (me) us in Jesus name Amen.

False Religion/Religious Spirits

✦ ✦ ✦

Father, in the name of Jesus, I (we) confess and ask for your forgiveness for coming in contact or agreement with doctrine of demons, heresies and blasphemes against your word and truth, causing me(us) to receive another Spirit or Gospel.

Forgive me (us) Lord for I (we) have sinned. I (we) know if I (we) sin willfully after I (we) have received the knowledge of the truth, there remains no more sacrifice for sin. Now then it is no more I (we) that do it, but sin that dwells in me (us). I (we) ask that you would cleanse me (us) from exposing myself (ourselves), my family, and my acquaintances, and remove any and all heretical teachings, soul ties, doctrinal beliefs, ritualism, formalism. legalism, doctrinal obsession, seduction, fear of God, fear of hell, fear of loss of salvation, and religiosity.

Deliver my soul from any evil spirits.

I (we) know that to be removed from Him that called us not the grace of Christ unto another Gospel, which is not another, but there be some that trouble us, and would pervert the Gospel of Christ, but though we, or an angel from heaven preach any other Gospel unto us, then that which we have preached unto us, let him be accursed.

I (we) surrender my (our) will to you. Use me (us) to bring Glory to your name in this end-time hour. In Jesus name Amen!

GENERATIONAL CURSES

✦ ✦ ✦

Father, let us therefore come boldly unto the throne of grace, that we may obtain mercy, and find grace to help in time of need, to be set free from all generational curses that are causing habits, behaviors, and cycles to repeat in my (our) life.

I (we) declare that Jesus died on the cross of Calvary to set me (us) free from all curses. I (we) am covered by his blood, and satan has no more power over me or my family line.

I confess my sin known and unknown _____

_____.

I (we) repent for them right now in Jesus name. I (we) take back the legal ground I (we) have given the enemy and ask for your forgiveness of my (our) sin and the sin of my (our) forefathers.

I (we) break and renounce the power of every demonic curse that has been passed down through the sin and actions of my(our) forefathers back to ten generations.

I (we) break the power and hold of every curse that come over me (us) through broken relationships, disobedience, rebellion, demonic strongholds, psychic inheritance, bondages of control or manipulation, failure, fear, idolatry, addictions, death, destruction, poverty, rejection, bonds of inherited sickness, diseases, physical, emotional, mental, spiritual illness or any curses put upon me (us) and my family line as a result of sin, transgressions, iniquities, occult involvement, or sin of the flesh from any member of my family line dead or alive.

I (we) break and renounce all legal ground and every stronghold the enemy has over my (our) family line to be destroyed in Jesus name. I (we) surrender to Jesus Christ. I am (we are) redeemed, justified, sanctified, and cleansed. Satan, you no longer have any power to harass, hinder, stop or block my (our) family line through generational curses. I am loosed, set free, and cut off from every curse put upon my family line. Father, Thank You that You became a curse for me (us), so that I can be free from every curse. In Jesus name Amen!

IDOLATRY

✦ ✦ ✦

"I am the Lord your God, who brought you out of the land of Egypt, from the house of bondage."

"You shall have no other Gods before me. You shall not make yourselves any graven images or any likeness of anything that is in heaven above of that is in the earth beneath, or that is in the waters beneath the earth, you shall not bow down yourself unto them nor serve them: For I the Lord your God am a jealous God."

"Wherefore, my dearly beloved flee from Idolatry."

Now the works of the flesh are manifest which are these adultery, fornication, uncleanness, lasciviousness, idolatry, witchcraft, hatred, variance emulations, wrath strife, seditions (causing division), heresies, envy, murders, drunkenness, revel lings, and anything like that of which I have told you in the time past that, "They which do such things shall NOT inherit the Kingdom of God."

It shall come to pass in that day says the Lord of Hosts that, "I will cut off the names of the Idols out of the land and they shall be no more remembered." For rebellion is as the sin of witchcraft, and stubbornness is as of iniquity and idolatry.

The lofty looks of man shall be humbled and the haughtiness of men shall be bowed down, and the Lord alone shall be exalted in that day, and the Idols shall be utterly abolished.

"Little children keep yourselves from Idols." "Be not overcome of evil, but overcome evil with good."

Let every soul be subject unto the higher power, for there are no powers but of God the powers that be are ordained of God. Whosoever therefore resists the powers resists the ordinance of God, and they that resists shall receive to themselves damnation.

Do that which is good and you shall have praise of the same. Blessed are they that do my commandments that they might have the right to the Tree of Life and may enter in through the gates in the city."

"I Jesus have sent my Angels to testify unto you these things in the churches." I am the root and off spring of David, and the bright and morning star." "He which testifies of these thing says God, "surely I come quickly."

May the grace of our Lord Jesus Christ be with you all. Amen!

LUST/PERVERSION SPIRITS
✦ ✦ ✦

Father, in the name of Jesus I acknowledge my sin unto you, and my iniquity I have not hid. I said, "I will confess my transgressions unto the Lord." I don't really understand myself, for I want to do what is right, but I don't do it. Instead, I do what I hate so, I am not the one doing wrong, it is sin living in me that does it, and I know nothing good lives in me that is in my sinful nature. I will not let sin, therefore, reign in my mortal body, but put on the Lord Jesus Christ and make no provisions for the flesh to fulfill the lust thereof.

I renounce all strongholds of lust/perversion spirits over my sexual character that is operating out of my flesh and bringing me into captivity.

I loose myself from all lust, perversion, mind control, lewdness, fornication, sexual impurities, uncleanness, pornography, cybersex, homosexuality, masturbation, oral sex, sodomy sex, cross dressing, prostitution, pedophilia, and whoredom.

I break all spirits controlling my eyes, ears, hands, mind, memory, my tongue, and my feet, that is causing me to be filled with unrighteousness.

I command all spirits that are controlling me of filthiness, loneliness, promiscuity, wickedness, covetousness, maliciousness, envy, murder, debate, deceit, malignity, whispers, backbiters, haters of God, despiteful, proud, boaster, inventor of evil things, disobedient to parents, without understanding, a covenant breaker, without natural affection, implacable, and unmerciful, to Come Out!

I cast out all spirits of sexual abuse, molestation, rape, incest, controlling spirits, domination, manipulation, confusion, curses of abuse, deception, depression, a thief, a violator, and mental bondage, shame, guilt, distrust, and fear.

I sever these spirits at the root from operating in my mind, body, soul, and my emotions.

Satan, the Lord rebukes you!

You will no longer come to steal, kill and destroy my life, to cause me to do things which are not convenient against my body and God's Word.

I will not be tempted! There has no temptation taken me, but such as common to man, but God is faithful, who will not let me be tempted above that which I am able, but will with the temptation, also make a way to escape that I may bear it.

I plead the blood over my entire sexual character, my eyes, ears, hands, feet, tongue, my mind, body, soul, and emotions. I will walk in the spirit and not fulfill the lust of the flesh. In Jesus name Amen.

Mind Control

✦ ✦ ✦

Satan, you are a liar! You no longer have control over my mind, thoughts, will, or my emotions.

Father, you have not given me the spirit of fear but of power, love, and a sound disciplined mind.

I reject all the negative thoughts that the enemy is trying to plant in my mind. I delight in the law after the inward man, but I see another law in my members warring against the law of my mind, and bringing me into captivity to the law of sin which is in my members.

Satan, I command you in the name of Jesus to loose your hold on my mind now!

I renounce all evil thoughts, all demonic influences, all satanic bondages, fear, mind control, mind binding, mental bondage, memory recall, knowledge block, depression, suicide, oppression, doubt, confusion, mind idolatry, pride, intellectualism, and rationalizing.

I cast down every foul unclean sprit that is afflicting, oppressing and attacking my mind.

Satan, the Lord rebukes you! I take authority and submit my mind to God and resist the devil and he will flee.

Father, I repent for sometimes being alienated and enemies in my mind by wicked works, yet now have You reconciled me in my mind. I will not be conformed to this world, but I will be transformed by the renewing of my mind. I will think on whatsoever things are true, whatsoever things are honest, whatsoever things are just, whatsoever things are pure, whatsoever things are lovely, whatsoever things are of a good report. If there be any virtue, if there be any praise, I will think on these things. I will let this mind be in me that is also in Christ Jesus Amen.

MIND CONTROL/WITCHCRAFT
RENUNCIATION
✦ ✦ ✦

Have mercy upon me, O God, according to Your loving kindness, according unto the multitude of Your tender mercies, blot out my transgressions. Wash me thoroughly from my iniquity, and cleanse me from my sin, for I acknowledge my transgressions, and my sin is ever before me. It's against You, only You, have I sinned, and done this evil in Your sight: that you might be justified when you speak, and be clear when you judge.

In the name of Jesus, Father, You gave unto me power to tread on serpents and scorpions and over all the power of the enemy, and nothing shall by any means hurt me, You gave unto me the keys of the kingdom of heaven, and whatsoever I shalt bind on earth shall be bound in heaven. Whatsoever I shalt loose on earth shall be loosed in heaven.

I renounce any and all strongholds over my mind from spirits of mind control, domination spirits, occult involvement, witchcraft, voodoo, astrology, divination, rebellion enchantment, familiar spirits, observer of times, sorcery, black magic, white magic, charmer, tarot card reader, candle burning, soothsayers, necromancers, mental energy, mind reading, second sight, lying, manipulation, sexual sins and deceiving.

Father, if I have any part or do these things, they are an abomination unto You, and, Lord, because of these abominations, You, Lord my God, will drive me out from before You. If my soul turns after such and go whoring after them, You will set my face against that soul and will cut me off from among Your people.

Father, I ask for Your forgiveness for opening myself up to these spirits that I may have exercised knowingly or unknowingly, consciously or unconsciously toward myself or other people; my family, the church, religious leaders, coworkers, and any other acquaintances past or present from any group or organization involvement. _____ (name them)

I claim freedom and I receive complete deliverance from these spirits operating in my life.

I confess that Jesus Christ is Lord and I plead the blood over myself and no weapon that is formed against me shall prosper; and every tongue that shall rise against me in judgment You shalt condemn. "This is the heritage of the servants of the LORD, and their righteousness is of me, says the LORD."

I will submit my mind to a faithful creator, resist the devil and watch him flee. In Jesus name Amen!

PRIDE

✦ ✦ ✦

If my people, which are called by my name, shall humble themselves, and pray, and seek my face, and turn from their wicked ways, then will I hear from heaven and will forgive their sin and heal their land.

Father, let not the foot of pride come against me. Pride goes before destruction and a haughty spirit before a fall, man's pride shall bring him low. When pride comes, then comes shame, but with the lowly is wisdom. Lord, forgive me for thinking of myself higher than I ought to.

I was shaped in iniquity; and in sin did my mother conceive me.

Hide your face from my sin, and blot out all my iniquities. I will walk with a humble spirit, and seek after God with my soul, with fasting and praying. God will prepare my heart that it will return unto my bosom, and cause my ear to hear. He will grant me deliverance and I will keep my body and bring it into subjection, lest that by any means when I have preached to others I myself should be a castaway. In Jesus name Amen.

Rebellion

✦ ✦ ✦

Woe to the rebellious children, says the Lord, "That take counsel, but not of me; and that cover with a covering, but not of my spirit, that they may add sin to sin."

Let every soul be subject unto the higher powers, for there is no power but of God. The powers that be are ordained of God. Whoever, therefore, resists the power, resists the ordinance of God, and they that resist shall receive to themselves damnation. For rebellion is as the sin of witchcraft, and stubbornness, is as iniquity and idolatry.

He rules by His power forever; his eyes behold the nations. Let not the rebellious exalt themselves. God sets the solitary in families and brings out those which are bound with chains, but the rebellious shall dwell in dry land, because, that which may be known of God is manifested in them, for God has showed it unto them.

Yes, all of you should be subject one to another and be clothed with humility for God resists the proud and gives grace to the humble. Likewise you younger, submit yourselves unto the elders.

Put them in mind to be subject to principalities and powers to obey magistrates, to be ready for every good work. "If you are willing and obedient, you shall eat the good of the land, but if you refuse and rebel, you shall be devoured with the sword for the mouth of the Lord has spoken it!" In Jesus name Amen.

Renunciation
of Occult Spirits
✦ ✦ ✦

In the name of Jesus, I acknowledge my transgressions and my sin is ever before me.

I desire truth in the inward parts, and in the hidden parts make me to know wisdom.

Father, I confess and ask for your forgiveness for coming in contact or agreement with any occults knowing or unknowing.

I renounce and rebuke myself and my family from any and all evil curses that are operating in our lives from any person(s) of an occult, psychic powers, sorcery, divination, voodoo, enchantment, eastern cults, charms, religious idols, Martial Arts, Judo, Kung Fu, Karate, Free Masonry, candle burning, occult games, observer of times, bewitchment, witchcraft, love potions, physics prayers, horoscope, astrology, levitation, fortune telling, tarot cards, pendulum, fetishes, hand writing analysis, ESP, hypnotism, Ouija board, palmistry, automatic writing and spoken words over my life, and _____ (name them) that have been put upon me back to ten generations on both sides of the family.

Satan, I break every familiar spirit of control and witchcraft off of my (our) life.

Heavenly Father, we ask that You will loose us from these occult spirits, and You will come near to us in judgment, and You be a swift witness against the sorcerers.

Let him that loves cursing receive it unto himself because Christ has become a curse for us, so that we can be free from every curse. In Jesus name Amen.

WITCHCRAFT
✦ ✦ ✦

Father, I repent for all involvement of witchcraft and divination spirits knowing or unknowing.

Judge me, O Lord my God, according to your righteousness. You are my hiding place. You shall preserve me from trouble.

In the name of Jesus, for we wrestle not against flesh and blood, but against principalities, against powers, against the rulers of the darkness of this world, against spiritual wickedness in high places.

Father, I rebuke all spirits of false teachings, false prophecy, and perversion connected to Jezebel.

Woe to the women that sew pillows to all armholes and make kerchiefs upon the head of every stature to hunt souls! Will you hunt the soul of God's people? And will you save the souls alive that come unto you? Will you pollute God among his people for handfuls of barley and for pieces of bread to slay souls that should not die, and to save the souls alive that should not live? By you're lying to God's people that hear your lies.

The Lord says that He is against your pillows wherewith you there hunt the souls to make them fly, and He will tear them from your arms and will let the souls go, even the soul that you hunt to make them fly.

He will tear your kerchiefs and deliver his people out of your hands, and they shall not be in your hands anymore to be hunted, and you shall know that he is the Lord God almighty.

I loose myself from all control, domination, manipulation, witchcraft, divination, voodoo, black magic, white magic, psychic inheritance, sorcery, candle burning, idolatry, familiar sprits, pride, tarot cards, tea leaf, crystal balls, levitation, palm reading, astral projection, Ouija boards, astrology and any connected and related to the spirit of Jezebel and witchcraft.

I renounce and break every curse, chain, cycle, spell and spoken curse over my life.

I loose myself from any operations of witchcraft spirits of bondage. I plead the Blood of Jesus over my mind, body, emotions and soul, and submit my will to my Lord and Savior Jesus Christ.

In Jesus name Amen!

A CRY FOR HELP

✦ ✦ ✦

I cried out to God with my voice, and he gave his ear unto me.

In the day of my troubles I sought the Lord. My sores ran in the night, and did not cease.

My soul refused to be confronted. I remembered God and was troubled.

I complained, and my spirit was overwhelmed. I am so troubled that I cannot speak. I have considered the days of old, the years of ancient ties. I call to remembrance my song in the night. I commune with my own heart, and my spirit made a diligent search. Will the Lord cast me off forever? Will he be favorable anymore? Does his promise fail me forevermore?

Has God forgotten to be gracious to me? Has He in anger shut up his tender mercies?

I said, this is my infirmity, but I will remember the years of the right hand of the most high. I will remember the works of the Lord, Surely I will remember your wonders of old I will meditate also of all your works and talk of your doings.

You are the God that does wonders; you have declared your strength among the people.

Your way, O God, is in the sanctuary. Who is so great?

A God as our God, who hears our cry for help! Amen!

Psalm 77

A WOMAN TO BE DESIRED

✦ ✦ ✦

O my love, you are beautiful! Yes, pleasant as the lilies among thorns, so is my beloved among the daughters. You are all fair, my love, there is no spot in you.

My love you have eyes as doves bright as the morning star. Your hair within hairs that blend together as they make their way down the mountainside. Your face shining as the glow of the sun, your nose is as the tower of Lebanon which look towards Damascus.

Your teeth are like a flock of sheep that are even shorn, where every one of them bear twins and none is barren among them. Your lips are like a thread of scarlet, sweet as a drop of honey comb, soft as a bed of pillows with milk under your tongue and the smell of spices flowing out with your comely speech. Your temples are like a piece of a pomegranate within your hair. Your neck is like a tower of ivory, strong and beautiful.

Your two breasts are like two young roes that are twins. Your belly is like a heap of wheat set about the lilies. Your navel is like a round goblet which wants not liquor.

The joint of your thighs are like jewels, the work of the hands of a cunning craftsman.

Your frame is like a palm tree standing confident as the wind blows through it.

O how beautiful are your feet with shoes. How fair and pleasant are you my love.

You have ravished my heart, for you are my delight, my sister, my friend.

I am your beloved and you are mine Amen.

Song of Solomon

THE BEREAVED
+   +   +

Blessed are they that mourn for they shall be comforted. If in this life only I (we) have hope in Christ, I (we) of all men most miserable, but now is Christ risen from the dead and become the first fruits of them that sleep. Yes, though I (we) walk through the valley of the shadow of death, I (we) will fear no evil for You are with me (us), Your rod and staff they comfort me (us). You have given me (us) beauty for ashes, the oil of joy for mourning, the garment of praise for the spirit of heaviness, so I (we) will comfort my (our) heart and be established in every good word and work.

I (we) will not be ignorant concerning them which are asleep. I (we) will not be in sorrow, even as others which have no hope. I (we) believe that Jesus died and rose again, even so, them which also sleep in Jesus will God bring with him. For it is the word of the Lord that I (we) which are alive and remain unto the coming of the Lord shall not prevent them which are asleep, for the Lord himself shall descend from heaven with a shout with the voice of the archangel and with the trumpet of God, and the dead in Christ shall rise first. Therefore, I (we) will pray to God in a time when I (we) may be found, that we which are alive and remain shall be caught up together with them in the clouds to meet the Lord in the air, and so shall we ever be with the Lord.

Therefore, I (we) will not sleep as others do, but I (we) will watch and be sober, and in everything give thanks for this is the will of God in Christ Jesus concerning me (us). In Jesus name Amen.

ANOINTED HANDS
+ + +

Heavenly father, I (we) come to you in the name that is above every name, the name of Jesus Christ.

Bless these hands to be hands that will manifest your power that I may lay hands on the sick and they will recover. Let these hands bind up the broken hearted, to proclaim liberty to the captive, and the opening of the prison to them that are bound.

Let these hands be released to bring blessings to myself and others. Let these hands bind up the wounds of body, mind, and spirit. Grant unto your servant, that with all boldness I may speak your word by stretching forth my hands to heal, deliver with signs, wonders and miracles that can be done by these hands in the precious name of your Holy Child Jesus, and that every yoke shall be destroyed because of the anointing, that even such mighty works are wrought by these hands.

I receive supernatural provisions and abundance of continual supply by these hands. In Jesus name Amen.

GOD'S SUPREME LOVE

✦   ✦   ✦

Beloved, if God so loved us, we should also love one another. No man has seen God at any time.

If we love one another, God dwells in us, and His love is perfected in us. Therefore, we know that we dwell in Him, and he in us, because He has given us His Spirit. As we have known and do testify that the Father sent the Son to be the Savior of the world, so whosoever will confess that Jesus is the Son of God, God will dwell in him and they will dwell in God. We have also known and believed the love that God has toward us, then we know God is love.

Here is our love made perfect that we may have boldness in the Day of Judgment, because as he is so are we in this world. There is no fear in love, but perfect love casts out fear, because fear has torment. He that fears is not made perfect in love. We love God because he first loved us. If a man says, "I love God," and hates his brother, he is a liar for he that does not love his brother whom he has seen, how can he love God whom he has not seen? Hereby, we perceive the love of God, because he laid down his life for us, and we ought to lay down our lives for our brethren. Amen!

I John 4

HEALING

✦ ✦ ✦

Father, you are my Jehovah Rapha, my healer. Surely you have born my (our) grief and carried my (our) sorrows, yet we did esteem Him stricken, smitten of God and afflicted, but He was wounded for our transgressions, he was bruised for our iniquities, the chastisement of our peace was upon Him; and with His stripes we are healed.

Heal me, O Lord, and I shall be healed; save me and I shall be saved.

Satan, the Lord rebukes you!

I submit myself unto God and he will take sickness and disease away from the midst of me.

Satan, you will not succeed in your plans of sickness for my life. Christ has redeemed me out of your hands by the blood of the Lamb.

I renounce all _____
and command it to go!

I take authority over my body, that is the temple of the Holy Spirit, and I loose myself from all traces of

_____

Father, I know whatsoever things I desire when I pray, believe that I will receive them, and I shall have them. The word is near me, even in my mouth, and in my heart; that is, the word of faith, which we preached, that I will receive my healing by faith and await my outward manifestation. In Jesus name Amen.

HOUSE PRAYER

✦ ✦ ✦

Unless the Lord builds this house, our labor is in vain. As for me and my house, we will serve the Lord.

Father, in the name of Jesus, We come asking you to forgive our trespasses and sin, wash us and cleanse us for all unrighteousness. We come boldly to the throne of grace to obtain mercy and find grace to help us in a time of need.

Father, for the weapons of our warfare are not carnal, but mighty through God to the pulling down of strong holds, casting down imaginations, and every high thing that exalts itself against the knowledge of God in this house.

Satan, we cast down all your attacks, plans, plots, and schemes against the family in this house.

We take authority over this place. Satan, get out now! We have all power over all your power and the Blood of Jesus covers this place.

We bind all hindering, harassing spirits of strife, confusion, fear, anger, lust, evil influences and every satanic bondage. The Blood of Jesus covers every area of this place: the door posts, the threshold, every room, the floor, every closet, every wall, every crack, every corner, windows, basement, attic etc. (name your places)

We reject all your entrances, and we command you to leave now!

This house is a house of prayer. The spirit of God resides here, and where the spirit of the Lord is, there is freedom, peace, joy, faith, trust and love, that we may grow up with him in all things and we shall love the Lord our God with all our heart, and with all our soul and with all our might. We shall teach the word diligently unto our children and shall talk of them when we sit in our house and when we walk by the way and when we lie down and when we rise up. We shall bind them for a sign upon our hand and they shall be as frontlets between our eyes, and we shall write them upon the post of our house and our gates.

The Lord will fill this house with his glory, and in this place he will give us peace, and this house shall be greater than the former, because He has heard our prayers and have chosen this place to Himself for a house of sacrifice, and His eyes shall be open, and His ears attend unto the prayers that are made in this house. Amen!

I will not Fear
✦   ✦   ✦

The LORD is my light and my salvation, whom shall I fear? The LORD is the strength of my life, of whom shall I be afraid?

When the wicked, even my enemies and my foes, came upon me to eat up my flesh, they stumbled and fell.

Though a host should encamp against me, my heart shall not fear. Though war should rise against me, in this will I be confident.

Hear my voice, O God, in my prayer; preserve my life from fear of the enemy.

For God, you have not given me the spirit of fear; but of power, love, and a sound mind. There is no fear in love, dread does not exist, but full grown complete perfect love turns fear out of doors and expels every trace of terror. For fear brings with it the thought of punishment, and so whomever is afraid has not reached the full maturity of love and is not yet grown into loves complete perfection. Therefore, I will not fear, though the earth may be removed, and though the mountains be carried into the midst of the sea, I will not fear!

I cast down all imaginations of apprehension, sudden fear, dread, terror, horror, drawback, intimidation, nervousness, anxiety, phobia, paranoia, worry, insomnia, panic, torment, distrust, suspicion, persecution, fears, confrontation, hysteria, insomnia, restlessness, roving, headaches, fear of disapproval, fear of man, fear of judgment, fear of condemnation, fear of reproof, shaking, fear of the devil, and every hindering spirit controlled by fear. I render you powerless over my mind, and loose myself from all control and vexation from the spirit of fear.

I command the spirit of fear to come out! I decree freedom from all spirits of fear from operating in my life. I will not fear them which kill the body, but are not able to kill the soul, but rather fear him which is able to destroy both soul and body in hell. In Jesus name Amen.

A MAN OF VALOR
✦ ✦ ✦

My beloved, when I think of how I have loved you all my life and didn't know you; part of it was a promise, that I knew would come true one day.

My beloved, who is strong and the chief among ten thousand, your head shining like the most of fine gold. Your eyes are as the eyes of doves by the river waters washed with milk and fitly set. Your cheeks are as a bed of spices as sweet flowers.

Your mouth is most sweet dropping a smell of myrrh. Your lips soft as butter, with your teeth as a flock of sheep which go up from the washing where everyone bear twins, and there is not one barren among them. Your belly is as bright ivory overlaid with sapphires. Your hands are as gold rings set with beryl with a gentle touch that brings forth the power of love. Your legs are as pillars of marble set upon a socket of fine gold as the apple tree among the trees of the wood. So is my beloved among the sons. Yes! You are altogether lovely, you are my friend, and you are my beloved, and you are mine. Come, my beloved, let us go forth into the fields; let us lodge in the villages, let us get up early to the vineyards; let us see the vine flourish together while we watch the tender grapes appear. My beloved, there will I give you my love, and you will give me yours. Amen

Song of Solomon

My Savior
✦ ✦ ✦

Woe is me, of my mother that have born me as a woman of strife, A woman of contention to the whole earth! I have neither lent on usury. Yet, every one of them did curse me.

O Lord, you know me quite well, remember me, visit me, and revenge me of my persecutors. Don't take me away from your longsuffering. Know this, that for your sake I have suffered rebuke. Your words were found in me, and I did eat of them. Your word brought unto me the joy and rejoicing of my heart. I was called by your name, O Lord God of hosts. I did not sit with the assembly of the mockers, nor did I rejoice with them. I sat alone because of your hand. You filled me with indignation. Why is my pain perpetual? And my wound is incurable? Which refuse to be healed? Will you be altogether to me as a liar?

And as water that fail? Therefore, I will say to the Lord, "I have returned."

If I have returned, then you, Lord, will bring me again and you shall stand before me.

And if you take forth the precious from the vile, you shall be as my mouth.

The Lord says, "Let them return to me, but you do not return unto them."

I will make you unto this people a fenced brazen wall and they shall fight against you, but they shall not prevail against you. "For I am with you to save you, to deliver you," says the Lord. "I will deliver you out of the hand of the wicked, And I will redeem you out of the hand of the terrible, says God." Amen

Jeremiah 15

NO REGRETS

✦ ✦ ✦

I Love the Lord, because he has heard my voice and my supplications. Because he has inclined his ear unto me, therefore, I will call upon him as long as I live.

The sorrows of death compassed me, and the pains of hell got hold of me.

I found trouble and sorrow. Then I called upon the name of the Lord.

O Lord, I Beg you deliver my soul. Lord you are gracious and righteous. Yes, you God are merciful. You, Lord, preserves the simple.

I was brought low and He helped me. He returned rest unto my soul; For the Lord has dealt bountifully with me. For he has delivered my soul from death, my eyes from tears, my feet from falling. I will walk before the Lord in the land of the living; therefore, I believed, I have spoken. I was greatly afflicted. I said in my haste, all men are liars. What shall I render unto the Lord for all His benefits toward me?

I will take the cup of salvation and call upon the name of the Lord. I will pay my vows unto theLord now in the presence of all his people. O Lord, I am truly your servant, I am your servant, you have loosened my bonds. I will offer to you the sacrifices of thanksgiving, and I will call upon the name of Lord. I will pay my vows unto the Lord now in the presence of all his people, in the courts of the Lords house in the midst of You. Praise You, the Lord! Amen!

Psalm 116

POWER OF PRAISE

✦ ✦ ✦

Let my prayer be set forth before You as incense and the lifting up of my hands as the evening sacrifice. I praise You, O Lord. O God, I will praise Your name. O God, I will praise Your name. I will sing unto you a new song and praise you in the congregation. I will praise You, for I am fearfully and wonderfully made, marvelous are your works and that my soul knows it quite well. I will praise You according to Your excellent greatness.

O Lord, our Lord, how excellent is Your name in all the earth!

You have set your Glory above the heavens. I will praise You with my whole heart.

I will show forth all your marvelous works, I will be glad and rejoice in You.

I will sing praises to your name. I will praise You with the harp, and sing to You with the psaltery and an instrument of ten strings. I will sing unto you a new song. I will play skillfully with a loud noise. I will make your name to be remembered in all generations, many shall see it, princes, judges, both young men and old men, women and children and all the people shall praise You. While I live I will praise You, Lord. You exalt the horn of your people, the princes of all your saints. Let us rejoice in You and praise your Holy name. I will praise You for your mighty acts, praise You according to your excellent greatness; praise You with the sound of instruments, praise You with timbel and dance. Let everything that has breath praise You the Lord, for it is pleasant and praise is comely, so every day, I will bless You and praiseYou for ever and ever.

Amen!

Prayer for Trials

✦ ✦ ✦

Father, I pray that You would move our enemies to depart from us; for we wrestle not against flesh and blood, but against principalities, against powers, against rulers of darkness of this world, against spiritual wickedness in high places.

God, I pray that You would break the weapon and the battle against us and that the spirit of the Lord will lift up a standard against the enemy.

God, we ask that You would preserve our soul and deliver us from the hand of the wicked.

We ask that You would give us power over all the power of the enemy, and that your eye would be upon the Body of Christ and your leaders, for the weapons of our warfare are not carnal but mighty through God, to the pulling down of strong holds, casting down imagination and every high thing that exalts itself against the knowledge of God and that no weapon formed against us shall prosper, for the battle is not ours but God's. Therefore, I will long for my joy and crown and stand fast in the Lord. In Jesus name Amen.

Restoration for Marriage
✦   ✦   ✦

Father, I (we) come to you for my (our) marriage, You promised that if we ask anything according to Your will that You hear us and that whatsoever we ask, we know that we have the petition we desire of You.

I (we) acknowledge my (our) sins unto You and my (our) iniquity I (we) have not hid. I (we) confess my (our) transgressions unto You, Lord, and You forgive the iniquity of my (our) marriage and restore unto us the joy of your salvation.

Father, I (we) know that marriage is honorable in your sight, and that my (our) struggle is not against a human opponent; but against rulers, against authorities, against cosmic powers in the darkness around us, against evil spiritual forces in the heavenly realm.

My (our) battle is with spiritual forces of darkness attacking my (our) marriage.

I (we) know that it is Your will, Father, that not any marriage end in divorce. I (we) want to please You, Lord, and walk in total obedience to You in my (our) marriage.

In the name of Jesus, I use the power and authority You have given me in Your name to rebuke and bind satan and every evil force attacking my (our) marriage of: rejection, anger, rage, unforgiveness, resentment, lies, fear, bitterness, retaliation, self-pity, shame, hindering spirits, addiction, infidelity, and contention.

I (we) decree freedom from suffering, bad memories, deep hurt, pain, sadness, and freedom over our finances.

I (we) loose love, joy, peace, longsuffering, gentleness, truth, trust and patience.

Father, by faith I (we) believe you heard our prayer for this marriage, and that it will be totally healed and restored, that we will submit ourselves one to another in the fear of God, for we are members of His body, of His flesh and His bones. My (our) marriage should be honored by all, and the marriage bed is kept pure (undefiled). In Jesus name Amen!

SALVATION

✦ ✦ ✦

Heavenly Father, The word of faith is in my mouth, that whosoever shall call upon the name of the Lord shall be saved, and if I shall confess with my mouth the Lord Jesus and shall believe in my heart that God has raised him from the dead, I shall be saved. With my heart I believe unto righteousness and with my mouth confession is made unto salvation.

I believe that Christ died for my sins according to the scripture and that he was buried and that he rose again on the third day according to the scripture.

I confess that I am a sinner. Please come into my heart. I accept you as my Lord and Savior. I repent of my sins, fill me with your love and your spirit, heal my body and deliver my soul and set me free. I know that God so loved the world that He gave His only begotten son, that whosoever believes in Him should not perish, but have everlasting life.

Thank you for justifying me, redeeming me, forgiving me, and cleansing me from all unrighteousness. May grace be with all who love our Lord Jesus Christ in sincerity. Amen!

THANKSGIVING

✦ ✦ ✦

I will bless the Lord at all times. His praises shall continually be in my mouth. I will offer a sacrifice of thanksgiving, and praise Him with my whole heart.

I will enter into His gates with thanksgiving and into His courts with praise and be thankful onto Him and bless His name.

Thank you, Lord, for healing me, delivering me from my secret faults, and covering all my sins with love. Thank You for restoring my soul and leading me in the path of righteousness for Your name sake; Thank You Lord; for I know You own a cattle upon a thousand hills, and there is no good thing, that you will withhold from them that walk upright before You. So, I will continue to give You thanks for all Your blessings and wondrous works.

My heart is fixed . . . My heart is fixed to always give You praise and thanksgiving. I will speak to You in psalms, hymns, spiritual songs, singing, and making melody in my heart to You, Lord.

I will continue to give thanks always for all things unto God and the Father in the name of our Lord Jesus Christ. Amen!

THE DELIGHT OF MY SOUL

✦ ✦ ✦

Father, I praise you for I am fearfully and wonderfully made. Marvelous are your works, my soul knows quite well. My soul shall be joyful in the Lord. It shall rejoice in Your salvation. O Lord, when shall I come and appear before you? My soul longs yes; it even faints for the courts of You, Lord. My heart and my flesh cries out for the living God. O Lord my God, in you do I put my trust. I pray, God, that my whole spirit, soul, and body be preserved blameless in the coming of our Lord Jesus Christ, as the hart pants after the water brooks, so pants my soul after You. O God, You restore my soul; You lead me in the path of righteousness for Your name sake.

Wherefore, I will lay apart all filthiness and superfluity of naughtiness and receive with meekness the engrafted word which is able to save my soul. For the word of God is quick, powerful, and sharper than any two-edged sword, piercing even to the diving asunder of soul and spirit, and the joints, morrow and is a discerner of the thoughts and intent of the heart. So, I will commit to keeping my soul to You in well doing as unto a faithful creator, and with patience I will possess my soul and love you with all my heart, all my soul, with all my mind and with all my strength. In Jesus name Amen!

The Lord's Prayer
✦   ✦   ✦

When you pray you shall not be as the hypocrites are. They love to pray standing in the synagogues and on corners of the streets that they may be seen of men, but when you pray enter into your closet, and after you have shut your door, pray to your Father which is in secret, and your Father which see in secret shall reward you openly.

When you pray do not use vain repetitions as the heathens do, don't be like them. Therefore, your Father knows what things you have need of before you ask Him.

One of Jesus's disciples came to him and asked," Lord teach us to pray." Jesus gave the disciple a model prayer to follow and to be used as a pattern for their prayer. Jesus said, "After this manner there pray you."

Our Father which art in heaven, Hallowed be thy name.

Thy kingdom come, Thy will be done in earth, as it is in heaven.

Give us this day our daily bread.

And forgive us our debts, as we forgive our debtors.

And lead us not into temptation, but deliver us from evil:

For thine is the kingdom, and the power, and the glory,

For if ye forgive men their trespasses,

your heavenly Father will also forgive you:

But if ye forgive not men their trespasses,

neither will your Father forgive your trespasses.

Forever amen!

THE NAME OF JESUS
✦ ✦ ✦

Jesus, by faith, I take full possession of the power and authority You have given me, that if I ask anything in Your name You will do it, that the father may be glorified in the Son.

From this day forward, I will go forth in Your name. I will go and teach all nations, baptizing them in the name of the father, and the son, and the Holy Spirit in the name of Jesus.

I will manifest that power that is in Your name. I will use it to proclaim salvation, to heal the sick, to cast out demons, to take authority over Satan, and take dominion in the earth!

Thank You that your name is above every name that in (at) the name of Jesus every knee should (must) bow, in heaven and on earth and underneath, and every tongue (frankly and openly) shall confess and acknowledge that Jesus Christ is Lord and to the Glory of God the Father.

Your name is far above all principality and power and might and dominion, and every name that is named, not only in this world but also in that which is to come.

Thank You for redeeming me, and saving me with the price You paid to obtain the power in that name by faith right now. I will have the confidence and boldness with power and authority You have given me to use your name, Jesus, Jesus, Jesus. Amen!

Trust

✦ ✦ ✦

The Lord is my shepherd, and I shall not want.

He makes me to lie down in green pastures: he leads me beside the still waters.

He restores my soul. He leads me in the paths of righteousness for his name's sake.

Yes, though I walk through the valley of the shadow of death, I will fear not evil;

For you are with me; your rod and your staff they comfort me.

You prepared a table before me in the presence of my enemies;

You anointed my head with oil; my cup runs over. Surely goodness and mercy shall follow me all the days of my life, and I will dwell in the house of the Lord forever. Amen

Psalm 23

Virtous Wife

✦   ✦   ✦

Who can find a virtuous woman with a price far above rubies?

My beloved husband, whom I safely trust, I will love you all the days of my life.

I will do you good and not evil, so that you will have no need of anything.

I will look well to the ways of my household; I will not eat the bread of idleness.

I am willing to work with my hands like the merchants.

Let me have the fruit of my hands. Let my own works praise me in the gates as I bring food from afar to eat. I will rise early while it is still night and prepare food for the household. I will gird my loins with strength, and strengthen my arm. I will stretch my hands to the poor, the needy, the widowed and the orphans. I am not afraid of bad weather, for my household, we are covered with scarlet as with the blood of Jesus.

I will make myself a covering of tapestry with my clothing made of silk and purple.

My love, you will be known in the gates when you are sitting among the elders of the land. Strength & honor will cover me as a garment, and I shall walk with joy in the time to come. I will open my mouth with wisdom, and my tongue will only speak of the law of kindness. Our children will rise up and call me blessed, and you, my love, will praise me.

Many daughters have done virtuously, but I will excel them all. Favor is deceitful, beauty is vain, but a woman who fears the Lord shall be praised. Amen

Proverbs 31

Waiting

✦ ✦ ✦

Truly my soul waits upon God; from Him comes my salvation.

He is only my rock and my salvation; He is my defense; I shall not be greatly moved.

My soul waits only upon God; for my expectation is from Him.

He is only my rock and my salvation; He is my defense; I shall not be moved.

In God is my salvation and my glory; the rock of my strength and my refuge is in God.

I will trust him at all times; I will pour out my heart before Him.

God is a refuge for me. God has spoken once; twice I have heard this that power belongs to God. Amen!

Psalms 62

WALKING IN GOD'S POWER
✦ ✦ ✦

Father, I will walk by faith and not by sight. You gave me the power to speak to the mountain and it shall be moved, and nothing shall be impossible unto me. Even so, faith if it has not works is dead alone; faith without works is dead.

If we have not used this power, but suffer all things lest we should hinder the gospel of Christ.

For the Kingdom of God is not in word but power, and this power may be of God and not of us. God is my strength and power, and He makes my way perfect that I can tread upon serpents and scorpions and over all the power of the enemy and nothing shall by any means hurt me. and This is the exceeding greatness of this power to us ward who believe according to the working of his mighty power so, I will be strong in the Lord and in the power of His might to heal the sick and cast out devils with the power and authority He has given me in heaven and in earth.

To teach all nations baptizing them in the name of the Father and of the Son and of the Holy Ghost, teaching them to observe all things whatsoever You have commended us in Jerusalem, in all Judea, in Samaria and in the uttermost parts of the earth. In Jesus name Amen.

PRAYER OF CONFESSION
✦ ✦ ✦

Father, in the name of Jesus on this day _____,
_____, at _____, your Word says, "If
we confess our sins, you are faithful and just to forgive us
our sins and to cleanse us from all unrighteousness."

I confess my sin of: _____

O Lord, have mercy upon me, O God, according to
your loving kindness; according unto the multitude of
your tender mercies, blot out my transgressions, wash me
thoroughly from my iniquity, and cleanse me from my sin.
For I acknowledge my transgression; and my sin is ever
before me. It's against You and only You I have sinned and
done this evil in Your sight, that You might be justified
when You speak and be clear when You judge.

I acknowledge my sin unto you and my iniquity I have
not hid. I will confess my transgression unto you Lord and
you forgive the iniquity of my sin.

Thank You, Lord, for delivering my soul in peace from
the battle that was in me. In Jesus name Amen!

Prayer of Petition

✦ ✦ ✦

I (we) petition Jesus Christ our Lord and Savior on this day, _____ at _____ for complete deliverance from the bondage of _____.

I John 5:14-15 says, "This is the confidence that we have in you, that if we ask anything according to your will you hear us, and if we know that you hear us, whatsoever we ask we know that we have the petition that we desire of you." Matthew 18:19 says, "Again I say unto you, that if two of you shall agree on earth as touching anything, that they shall ask it shall be done for them of my Father which is in heaven." Matthew 18:18 says, "Verily I say unto you, whatsoever you shall bind on earth shall be bound in heaven and whatsoever you shall loose on earth shall be loosed in heaven."

I (we) petition in the name of Jesus that you will bind the enemy from putting a yoke of _____ around my neck and loose the blood of Jesus over me (us) and the peace of God that surpasses all understanding.

I (we) petition and bombard the gates of Hell that they may know that this is Your hand that You Lord have done it.

I (we) petition that you would sever the cord of the enemy from _____, and I (we) decree it done believing and standing in agreement that this petition will be passed in Jesus name. Amen.

_____   _____

Signature   Date

_____   _____

Witness Signature   Date

Promises of God

✦ ✦ ✦

I command you this day that the Lord your God will set you on high above all nations of the earth. If you shall hearken diligently unto the voice of the Lord your God to observe and do all his commandments and all these blessings shall come on you and overtake you if you shall hearken unto the voice of the Lord your God.

Blessed shall you be in the city, and blessed shall you be in the field. Blessed shall be the fruit of your body and the fruit of your ground. Blessed shall you be when you come in and blessed shall you be when you go out.

Blessed are the poor in spirit for their is the kingdom of heaven. God is with men, and he will dwell with them, and they shall be his people, and God himself shall be with them, and be their God.

Blessed are they that mourn for they shall be comforted, beauty for ashes, the oil of joy for mourning, the garment of praise for the spirit of heaviness.

Blessed are the meek for they shall inherit the earth. Better it is to be of a humble spirit with the lowly than to divide the spoil with the proud.

I will make you a great nation, and I will bless you, and make your name great, and you shall be a blessing. I will bless them that bless you and curse them that curses you and in you shall all families of the earth be blessed.

Blessed are they which do hunger and thirst after righteousness for they shall be filled; for only the righteous shall see God.

Blessed are the merciful for they shall obtain mercy. It is of the Lord's mercies that we are not consumed because his compassion (mercy) fails not; they are new every morning.

Blessed are the pure in heart for they shall see God. He that has clean hands and a pure heart who has not lifted up his soul unto vanity nor sworn deceitfully, he shall receive the blessings from the Lord and righteousness for the God of his salvation.

Blessed are the peace makers for they shall be called the children of God. Follow peace with all men and holiness, without which no man shall see the Lord.

Blessed are they which are persecuted for righteousness sake, for this the kingdom of heaven; trust in the Lord with all your heart and lean not to your own understanding in all your ways. Acknowledge him and he shall direct your path.

Blessed are you when men shall revile you and persecute you and shall say all manner of evil against you falsely for my sake. Rejoice and be exceedingly glad for great is your reward in heaven.

Blessed is the man that walks not in the counsel of the ungodly, nor stands in the way of sinners, nor sit in the seat of the scornful. But his delight is in the law of the LORD, and in his law does he meditate day and night. And he shall be like a tree planted by the rivers of water that brings forth his fruit in his season. His leaf also shall not wither, and whatsoever he does shall prosper.

The LORD shall command the blessing upon you in your storehouses, and in all that you set your hand to; and he shall bless you in the land which the LORD your God gives you. The LORD shall establish you a holy people unto Himself, as he has sworn unto you, if you shall keep the commandments of the LORD your God, and walk in his ways. And all people of the earth shall see that you are called by the name of the LORD; and they shall be afraid of you. And the LORD shall make you plenteous in goods, in the fruit of your body, and in the fruit of your cattle, and in the fruit of your ground, in the land which the LORD swore unto your fathers to give you. The LORD shall open unto you his good treasure, the heaven to give the rain unto your land in his season, and to bless all the work of your hands, and you shall lend unto many nations, and you shall not borrow. And the LORD shall make you the head, and not the tail; and you shall be above only, and you shall not be beneath.

Blessed are they that do His commandments that they may have the right to the Tree of Life and may enter in through the gates in to the city.

"My Word that goes forth out of my mouth, it shall not return unto me void, but it shall accomplish that which I please, and it shall prosper in the things whereto I sent it."

For all the promises of God in Him are yes, and in Him Amen, unto the Glory of God by us.

In Jesus name Amen!

Covenant Agreement
+ + +

I _____ make this covenant with the Lord God almighty. This day _____ of _____, 20_____.

I will not be rash with my mouth and let my heart be hasty to utter anything before God in heaven.

When I vow this vow unto God and defer not to pay it, he has no pleasure in fools. I will not let my mouth cause my flesh to sin. Ecclesiastes 5:2, 6

I, therefore enter into this covenant with the Lord who is God that made heaven and earth. I commit my life to seek His face and His direction for my life.

I will make this covenant with God to accept the call which He has chosen for me in Him before the foundation of the world, that I should be holy and without blame before Him in love.

I will take more time to learn of Him to become His co-labor with Him for the Kingdom of God.

Signed _____ Date _____

Witnessed_____ Date _____

BIOGRAPHY
✦ ✦ ✦

Marla D. Whittington *of Chicago, Illinois, a licensed and ordained anointed, extraordinary, heartfelt speaker and teacher. The founder of Daughters of Zion Women Ministries; Pastor Marla proclaims a powerful message of healing, restoration and deliverance to God's people. The Lord has given Marla the tongue of the learned that she should know how to speak a word in season. (Isaiah 50:4a) She also preaches a message of salvation and hope to the lost. Pastor Marla travels around the country declaring the gospel of Jesus Christ. She has ministered at many conferences; conducted shut-ins, and seminars, participated in several mission trips, and training to help build up leaders into the body of Christ. The Word of God says, "The greatest among you will be a servant to all". Pastor Marla enjoys serving wherever God sends her. She has served with many Non-for-Profit Organizations. She is rapidly emerging as one of the world's most prolific speakers and teachers of the Word of God. The Lord has strengthened Pastor Marla by His grace to stand in the midst of trials. God uses what she has experienced in her own life to strengthen and build up others. The Word of God says this about her; "The Lord has called me from the inward part of my mother. He has made mention of my name, and he has made my mouth like a sharp sword; in the shadow of His hand, he has hidden me, and made me a polished shaft. He said to me; you are my servant whom I will be glorified". (Isaiah 49:1-3) She has received her Bachelors of Arts Degree in Christian Education at Shalom Bible College in Wes Des Moines, Iowa She is also the mother of Son LuVince IV, daughter La Trice, Son Lamar and the grandmother of 6.*